LiFE iN SHANNONDALE

GOATiE

THE B-A-A-A-D GOAT

DEAN PARRISH

WestBow Press books may be ordered through booksellers or by contacting:

WestBow Press
A Division of Thomas Nelson & Zondervan
1663 Liberty Drive
Bloomington, IN 47403
www.westbowpress.com
844.714.3454

ISBN: 978-1-6642-0522-2 (sc)
ISBN: 978-1-6642-0524-6 (hc)
ISBN: 978-1-6642-0523-9 (e)

Library of Congress Control Number: 2020917505

Print information available on the last page.

WestBow Press rev. date: 09/11/2020

WESTBOW
P R E S S®
A DIVISION OF THOMAS NELSON
& ZONDERVAN

LIFE IN SHANNONDALE

GOATiE

THE B-A-A-A-D GOAT

Meet Lisa Marie. Lisa lives on a farm in Shannondale. She loves animals and she loves adventure.

Lisa helps Uncle Earl and Aunt Laura Sue with chores on the farm.

One day, Lisa Marie brought home a new baby goat. She named him Goatie.

A few days later, the weather got really cold outside so Lisa wanted to bring Goatie inside to keep him warm. Goatie had never felt anything like this. The fire was warm and it felt so good that Goatie wanted to get closer.

Goatie got too close and his tail caught fire! The fire did not feel so good anymore. Goatie ran around the room and jumped on the table. Lisa Marie threw water on Goatie to put out the fire.

"Bad goat!" said Lisa Marie.

"B-a-a-a-a-d!" said Goatie.

Goatie loved playing with the boys and girls who lived near the farm and they loved playing with him. Goatie would watch them get on the school bus every day, and then would be there waiting when they got off the bus.

One day, when the kids got on the bus, Goatie jumped on the bus and ran all the way to the back of the bus! Everyone was running and jumping and trying to catch Goatie. Lisa Marie ran out to the bus and caught Goatie.

"Bad goat!" said Lisa.

"B-a-a-a-d!" said Goatie.

A few days later, a truck pulled into the drive with a box for Lisa. Goatie jumped into the truck and ran away with the man's drink cup! Lisa Marie ran after Goatie to get the cup, but Goatie ate it.

"Bad goat!" said Lisa.

"B-a-a-a-a-d!" said Goatie.

Lisa Marie told Aunt Laura Sue she needed help to keep Goatie out of trouble.

"Maybe you should get another goat," Aunt Laura Sue told Lisa.

The next day, Uncle Earl brought a new goat to Lisa to be a friend for Goatie. Lisa named the new goat Rhonda after the lady who sold the goat to Uncle Earl.

Goatie and Rhonda the Goat ran around the barn and in the field, chasing each other and playing.

Maybe having a new friend will keep Goatie out of trouble, Lisa thought.

The very next morning, Lisa Marie went out to get on her golf cart to do her chores.

When Lisa stepped outside, Goatie was sitting at the steering wheel on the golf cart and Rhonda the Goat was standing under the steering wheel. Rhonda jumped when she saw Lisa coming and stepped on the gas pedal. The golf cart took off with Goatie at the wheel and Rhonda pushing the gas! Lisa ran after them, but tripped over one of the dogs.

While Lisa was on the ground with a dog licking her face, the geese came over honking and flapping their wings to chase the dogs away. All the noise scared Rhonda and she jumped off the golf cart. The cart stopped just before it ran into the side of the house.

"Bad goat!" said Lisa.

"B-a-a-a-d!" said Goatie.

Lisa drove the cart into the barn and turned off the key. Lisa looked at Goatie and laughed.

"I love you, Goatie," said Lisa. "And I love life in Shannondale."

Printed in the United States
By Bookmasters